The Story of Harley-Davidson

Josepha Sherman

Mitchell Lane
PUBLISHERS

P.O. Box 196
Hockessin, Delaware 19707
Visit us on the web: www.mitchelllane.com
Comments? email us: mitchelllane@mitchelllane.com

Mitchell Lane
PUBLISHERS

A Robbie Reader

Albert Einstein	Alex Rodriguez	Barbara Park
Charles Schulz	Dale Earnhardt Jr.	Donovan McNabb
Dr. Seuss	Henry Ford	Hilary Duff
Jamie Lynn Spears	Johnny Gruelle	LeBron James
Mia Hamm	Philo T. Farnsworth	Robert Goddard
Shaquille O'Neal	**The Story of Harley-Davidson**	Syd Hoff
Thomas Edison	Tony Hawk	

Library of Congress Cataloging-in-Publication Data
Sherman, Josepha.
     The story of Harley-Davidson / by Josepha Sherman.
         p. cm. — (A Robbie reader)
     Includes bibliographical references and index.
     ISBN 1-58415-358-X (library bound)
1. Harley-Davidson motorcycle—History—Juvenile literature. 2. Harley-Davidson Incorporated—History—Juvenile literature. I. Title II. Series.
TL448.H3S46 2005
629.227'5'0973—dc22
                                   2004030512

ABOUT THE AUTHOR: Josepha Sherman is a professional fantasy and science fiction writer, a *Star Trek* novelist, a children's writer, and a nonfiction writer with over 60 books in print and over 150 short stories. She is also a professional folklorist and editor. In addition, she is a native New Yorker, has a degree in archaeology, loves to tinker with computers, follows the NY Mets ("wait till next year!"), and is a horse whisperer who has had a new foal fall asleep on her foot!

PHOTO CREDITS: Cover: Barbara Marvis; p. 4 Harley-Davidson Archives; p. 6 Library of Congress.; pp. 8 Harley-Davidson Archives; p. 10 Jamie Kondrchek; p. 12 Corbis; p. 14 Collections of Henry Ford Museum and Greenfield Village; pp. 16, 18 Corbis; p. 20 Library of Congress; p. 22 Getty Images; pp. 23, 24 Barbara Marvis; p. 26 Randy Lagana

ACKNOWLEDGMENTS: The following story has been thoroughly researched, and to the best of our knowledge, represents a true story. While every possible effort has been made to ensure accuracy, the publisher will not assume liability for damages caused by inaccuracies in the data, and makes no warranty on the accuracy of the information contained herein. This story has not been authorized nor endorsed by anyone associated with Harley-Davidson.

TABLE OF CONTENTS

Chapter One
A Very Strange Factory 5

Chapter Two
The Two Friends 9

Chapter Three
A Company Grows 13

Chapter Four
Changes 19

Chapter Five
Harley-Davidson Today 25

Chronology 29-30
Glossary 30
To Find Out More 31
Index 32

This is the shed that housed the Harley-Davidson company when it was first started. It was light enough for four men to pick it up and move.

In this picture, the shed is in the shadow of a more modern version of the Harley-Davidson factory.

A Very Strange Factory

In Wisconsin in the 1900s, there was only one way to get anywhere in a hurry. That was the railroad. But the railroad didn't run everywhere that people wanted to go.

The people who were in charge of building new rails looked at the city of Milwaukee. It didn't look too much like a city. There were dirt streets. There were houses without electricity. But if the railroad went through Milwaukee, it might bring more money into the city. That would mean more

This photo was taken about 1900. It shows two steam
locomotives, the best and fastest type of transportation of that
time. Some of the steam powering the engines can be seen
coming out of the smokestack on the locomotive on the left.

people could afford to use the railroad. That would make more money for the railroad.

Only one building stood in the way. It was the Harley-Davidson factory. The railroad people went to see the factory.

All they found was a shed. On its door was a hand-drawn sign. It said, HARLEY-DAVIDSON FACTORY. Four men came running. Three of them were very young. They were, they said, Arthur Davidson, his brother Walter, their father, and William Harley. When they found out what the railroad people wanted, each of the four men went to one wall of the shed. They picked up the shed and moved it to a new spot.

The railroad people thought that such a small company could never become important.

They were wrong.

Here is a group portrait of Harley-Davidson's founders, taken in 1912. From left to right, they are Arthur Davidson, Walter Davidson, William Harley, and William Davidson. They look pretty grim here, even though their new company was doing well.

The Two Friends

In 1900, two young men who lived in Milwaukee, Wisconsin, wanted a faster way to get around. Their names were William Harley and Arthur Davidson. William was born in 1880, and Arthur was born in 1881. They were good friends.

In those days, it wasn't unusual for boys to leave school as soon as they had learned how to read and write. They needed to go to work. Both William and Arthur left school when they were in their teens. William worked for a bicycle maker. He learned everything about bicycles and how they worked. Arthur worked for a company that made the **patterns**, or designs, for the parts of engines. In the early 1900s, engine parts were not sold in stores. They had to be specially made, following the right pattern.

This classic Harley motorcycle dates from 1907. It shows how the early machines looked more like bicycles than modern motorcycles. But there are no pedals. This is a true motor-driven machine.

When William was twenty-one and Arthur was twenty, they worked for the same company. The company made engine parts from patterns. The two friends knew all about bicycles by then. They knew all about making machine engines.

There were a few motorbikes in Milwaukee. Motorbikes were just bicycles with engines attached to them. The engine was often too strong for the bicycle. It would tear the bicycle's frame apart. William and Arthur decided to build something better, a frame and an engine that belonged together. They called their idea a **motorcycle**.

A motorcycle has two wheels like a bicycle. It can go over paved roads like an automobile. It can also go over dirt roads or even no roads at all. William and Arthur were sure that many people would want to buy their motorcycles.

William Davidson (left) and William Harley (right) found their company's product to be a perfect way to get out for an afternoon's fishing trip. While William Davidson drives, William Harley sits in the sidecar. That's quite a lot of fish the two men caught!

A Company Grows

William and Arthur began working on their new idea. They needed someone who knew more about designing engines. Arthur's brother, Walter, built machines. Arthur and William asked Walter to build them an engine for their motorcycle.

Walter liked the idea. It took William, Arthur, and Walter three years. Finally, in 1903, they had a motorcycle that worked. They built another, and another. That year, they sold their first motorcycle.

Their business needed a name. They decided to use their own last names. William wanted Arthur's name to go first. He said that Arthur had first thought about building a motorcycle. It was agreed: the new company would be called Harley-Davidson.

This is the first car Henry Ford built in 1896. It doesn't look at all like a modern automobile, more like a cart with a motor. It also didn't have a reverse gear, and couldn't go backwards.

Now they needed someone to sell their motorcycles. Arthur had another brother, who was also named William. This William wasn't really interested in motorcycles, but he knew how to run a business.

The new company sold two motorcycles in 1904. They sold eight in 1905. Word got out that the Harley-Davidson company built good machines. In 1906, they sold fifty motorcycles. Arthur's Aunt Janet liked the neat black machines, but she thought that they needed a little color. She painted thin red stripes on them. She also added a black-and-red badge. It became the official Harley-Davidson badge. It is still being used.

In 1903, Henry Ford opened the Ford Motor Company. His company made automobiles. They were very popular, and every year more and more people bought them. The Harley-Davidson company had to prove that motorcycles were also useful and

Walter Davidson poses with his bike after winning the 1908 Federation of American Motorcyclists' endurance run. It didn't take long after the brothers built their first motorcycle that they started winning races. This motorcycle looks less like a bicycle than the one built in 1907.

fun. They had to prove that their motorcycles wouldn't break down.

In 1908, Walter Davidson became the president of the Harley-Davidson company. He also was a terrific motorcycle rider. He raced their motorcycles and showed everyone how well they ran.

Arthur knew that the company needed good **mechanics**. He started a Harley-Davidson Service School to train those mechanics.

Advertising was important, too. People wouldn't buy Harley-Davidson motorcycles if they didn't know the motorcycles existed. Police departments were interested in buying motorcycles. Arthur ran special ads for them: "There Is Something Undeniably Right About a Cop on a Harley-Davidson." Many police departments agreed.

An employee works on the construction of a motorcycle engine at the Harley-Davidson plant. He's building it by hand. This was before the days of computers and modern means of building things.

Changes

The Harley-Davidson company was growing quickly. By 1912, there were so many people working for them that a new headquarters and factory were built. The motorcycles were starting to look less like bicycles and more like modern motorcycles. They could go at 45 miles per hour, faster than many automobiles back then. In fact, by 1914, the company officially entered motorcycle racing. In the following years, Team Harley-Davidson did so well that they were nicknamed the Wrecking Crew because they "wrecked" the chances anyone else had to win.

But 1914 was also the beginning of World War I. This was a huge war that lasted

Two men ride a Harley-Davidson motorcycle equipped with a side car. This is a much larger motorcycle than the one on page 12. The sidecar is more modern, too.

for four years. The United States, Great Britain, France, and other countries defeated Germany, Austria, and others. About a third of the motorcycles built by Harley-Davidson were bought and used by the U.S. military. By 1920, Harley-Davidson was the largest maker of motorcycles in the world. By 1930, only Harley-Davidson and one other U.S. company, Indian, were making motorcycles.

In 1937, a Harley-Davidson motorcycle set a speed record of 136 miles per hour. Sadly, this same year William Davidson died.

The United States found itself involved in another world war in 1941. World War II would last until 1945. During those four years, Harley-Davidson supplied over 90,000 motorcycles for the military.

Walter Davidson would not get to see the factory return to making civilian bikes at the end of the war. He died in 1942. A year later, in 1943, William Harley died of a heart attack.

A man puts an early Harley-Davidson motorcycle through its paces on a steep gradiant. It looks like the hill is winning. The bike and its rider are about to take a tumble.

In addition to building and riding motorcycles, Arthur enjoyed living on his farm. He raised a breed of cows called Guernsey cattle. Arthur also liked giving to charity. He helped organizations such as the Boy Scouts and a home for the blind in Wisconsin. Arthur and his wife died in an automobile accident in 1950.

By the 1960s, the outlook was grim for Harley-Davidson. The company was losing money. It couldn't keep up with the cheaper motorcycles from Japan, built by companies such as Kawasaki and Suzuki. Harley-Davidson also needed to update its whole way of doing business. In 1969, Harley-Davidson merged with the American Machine and Foundry Company (AMF). It was no longer its own company.

Here is a Harley sitting near Mike's Famous Harley-Davidson store in New Castle, Delaware. It shows how far motorcycle designs have come since the early twentieth century.

Mike's Famous Harley-Davidson is a store, but it also has a bike museum and a restaurant. Many Harley enthusiasts like to hang out here and talk about how much they like their bikes.

Harley-Davidson Today

The employees of Harley-Davidson didn't like being part of another company. On February 26, 1981, they announced that they were going to buy the Harley-Davidson Motor Company back from AMF. By the middle of June, they had officially gotten back their company. The news was announced around the company by the cry, "The Eagle Soars Alone."

Today, Harley-Davidson is a successful company again. More than 8,200 people around the world work for it. Anyone who is

Today, Harley riders can also take their pets on rides with them. The bikes and Yorkshire puppy belong to artist Randy Lagana and his wife, Jen. The puppy posing for this picture is named Pax.

curious about how motorcycles are made can take a factory tour. The Rider's Edge is the name of the Harley-Davidson Academy of Motorcycling. It offers training to riders of all levels. The Harley-Davidson Foundation helps people in all the areas in which there are Harley-Davidson plants. The **foundation** gives money for education, the arts, health care, and the environment.

Harley owners love their bikes. Many of them belong to a group called H.O.G., the Harley Owners Group. By 2005, H.O.G. had about 900,000 members.

Even those who aren't members of a group have good things to say about their bikes. An owner, Bob, says, "I like the style and the feel of the bike and you can always tell when one is coming. It's loud, exciting, and shakes your entire insides. You don't just ride the bike, it's a part of you."

Another owner, Peter, adds, "Harley is more than a motorcycle, it is an image."

And another owner, Randy, says, "There is a great sense of freedom and a carefree feeling. Anytime I am troubled by something, a motorcycle ride blows it right out of my head. I call it 'cycle therapy.'"

Randy's wife Jen also said, "There are a number of things that are awesome about riding. It is a very freeing feeling with the breeze in your hair. There is nothing better than taking the bikes out together [with my husband]. Now that we can take the dogs with us too, it is even better!

Harley owners have even created a list called "101 Reasons to Own a Harley." Some of these reasons are:

They're beautiful.
Even an old, beaten up one looks good.
Anyone can ride one.
[A Harley] can make you smile on a bad day.

1870 William Davidson is born.

1876 Walter Davidson is born.

1880 William Harley is born.

1881 Arthur Davidson is born.

1900 William Harley and Arthur Davidson decide to build motorcycles.

1903 The first Harley-Davidson motorcycle is sold.

1906 The first Harley-Davidson factory is built.

1908 Motorcycle racing begins.

1917 During World War I, Harley-Davidson builds military motorcycles.

1918 One-third of Harley-Davidson motorcycles are used by the U.S. military.

1937 William Davidson dies.

1941 The United States joins World War II.

1942 Walter Davidson dies.

1943 William Harley dies.

1945 By the end of World War II, Harley-Davidson has manufactured over 90,000 motorcycles for the military.

1950 Arthur Davidson dies.

1969 Harley-Davidson merges with AMF.

1981 Harley-Davidson executives buy back the company.

1993 Harley-Davidson's 90th Anniversary and Family Reunion attracts hundreds of thousands of riders.

2003 Harley-Davidson's 100th Anniversary is celebrated with great fanfare.

2005 Harley-Davidson motorcycles are selected to serve the Los Angeles, California Police Department.

GLOSSARY

advertising (AD-ver-ty-zing)—telling people about a person or product, usually on a large scale.

foundation (fown-DAY-shun)—an organization that helps people.

mechanic (meh-KAN-ik)—a person trained to work on machines such as cars or motorcycles.

motorcycle (MOW-ter sy-kuhl)—a two-wheeled motorized vehicle.

motorized bicycle (mow-TER-eyzd bye-sih-kuhl) a bicycle with a motor attached to it.

pattern (PAT-urn)—a design for something, such as a dress or a machine part.

Davidson, Jean. *Jean Davidson's Harley-Davidson Family Album: 100 Years of the World's Greatest Motorcycle in Rare Photos.* Stillwater, Minnesota: Voyager Press, 2003.

Davidson, Jean. *My Daddy Makes the Best Motorcycles in the Whole Wide World: The Harley-Davidson.* Woodruff, Wisconsin: Guest Cottage, Inc., 2004.

Norris, Martin. *Rolling Thunder.* London: Quintet Publishing, 1992.

Ready, Dean. *Motorcycles.* Minneapolis: Capstone Press, 1998.

Young, Jesse. *Harley-Davidson Motorcycles.* Minneapolis: Capstone Press, 1994.

Web Addresses

The Motorcycle Hall of Fame Museum
http://www.amadirectlink.com/museum/

The Official Harley-Davidson Web Site
http://www.harley-davidson.com/

Davidson, Arthur
  Birth of   9
  Charities   23
  Death of   23
  Farm life   22-23
  Works for engine
    maker   10
Davidson, Walter
  Becomes president
    of Harley-
  Davidson   17
  Builds engine for   13
  Death of   21
  Harley-Davidson   13
Davidson, William
  Death of   21
  Joins company   15
Ford, Henry   15
Ford Motor Company 15
Harley, William
  Birth   9
  Death   21
  Works for bicycle
    maker   9-10

Harley-Davidson
  Academy/Rider's Edge
    27
Harley-Davidson Company
  Badge   15
  Employees buy back
    company   25
  Enters motorcycle
    racing   19
  Factory 19
  First motorcycle   13
  Merges with American
    Machine and Foundry
    Company   23
  Name   14
Harley-Davidson
  Foundation   27
Harley-Davidson Service
  School 17
Harley-Davidson shed 7
H.O.G. (Harley Owners
    Group)   27
Milwaukee   5, 9
World War I   20
World War II   21
"Wrecking Crew, The" 20